Things Not Long Forgotten
Copyright © 2013 by De'Borah Raquel

Published by Swain~N~Company

Printed in the United States of America
All rights reserved. No part of this publication may be reproduced, stored in a retrieval system, or transmitted in any form or by any means, electronic, mechanical, photocopying, recording, or otherwise, without the prior written permission of the publisher.

Things Not Long Forgotten
By
De'Borah Raquel

I used to...

The Truth about Me

I realized
All I've ever wanted
From you for the seven years
That I've known you
Was for you to love me
It was easy to pretend
I didn't care
Or that I didn't need you
To be my friend
But on the inside
I felt like crying
Every time I was near you
And couldn't hold you
A part of me would just die
A little
And it hurt every time
I couldn't kiss you
So I cried a million tears
For the million kisses
I'd never get to give you
Probably don't care now
I wouldn't be able to live
With myself if I didn't
At least try
Once more
You're all that I could never
Leave behind
I hang on the thread
Of the moments
Waiting for you to love me
I do live just for that day
When you will care
You don't need me anymore
It's not as hard as I think
You're only my best friend
The one constant thing in my life
Who am I without you?
I'm lost

Like a puppet
Without a puppet master
I'll show you my devotion
Just give me the chance to
If you said "no"...
I would understand

Not in Love

"I'm not in love"
That's what I told myself
Time and time again
Always trying to walk away
Why should I deny myself
The way you steal glances
Fire in your eyes
Burning looks
I catch a glimpse
Of our love at winter's edge
We know we should be together
We just can't
Seem to figure out how
To make us work
Or maybe we don't want to
Perhaps we need the pain
To live or we think
We need it to survive
Press your lips softly
Against mine
Let out a gentle prayer
Kissing you is like
Inhaling fire covered in ice
Created to compliment
Perfectly natural
As our hands seek to join
Still I can't hold you
And if I had the chance
I wouldn't know how to show you
Just turn away from this
And believe
"I'm not in love"

Longing

I feel empty
I wrap myself in hollowness
Not wanting to feel at all
Needing to kiss him once more
The loneliest feeling
"I see no reason in feeling that way
For someone who doesn't
Feel that way for me"
The saddest words sung into my ears
The sweetest hurt in my heart
Surges of tears rise in my eyes
Swaying on the wings of despair
I lose myself to the pain
Lose my sanity in his eyes
My love for him so deep
It lies hidden
To the point that he can't see it
He let go of me
Now I must do the same for him
Though I need him
Just to breathe
Just to live a semi-normal life
Burying my face in his neck
Taking my comfort there
I've loved him for so long
And still do
He leaves me empty-handed
Until I am breathlessly
Longing

Natural Disaster

If some natural disaster
Should sweep you away
To a somewhat distant shore
I would spend the rest
Of my days
Pining for you
It would become
My deepest passion
To find you

Soothe the pain of longing
To see your face
Hear you breathing
Feel your heart beating
Hold you in my arms
Look into your eyes
Taste your kiss
What would I say
Just to hold you
Once more
For just one single
Solitary moment
But would you care
That I had traveled
So far and so long
Or would you be
Glad to know
How I filled myself
With you until I no longer existed
I wanted to die for you

Hate to Love You

I hate the power you have over me
I hate the way you manipulate my heart
With a single word
I hate when you make me whine your name
I hate the way you kiss me
With so much tenderness
I feel like I just can't take it
I hate the way I cry over you
Like there will not be a tomorrow
I hate the way you look at me
When you think I'm not aware
I hate it when you touch me and how it makes me feel
I hate how well you know me
From the look on my face to the thoughts I don't verbalize
Most of all
I hate the way I love you
Even though you break my heart
I hate the way you love me
Because it hurts so bad
But I let it happen anyway
Then I hate myself

Desire

Here, I find in you
My end and beginning
You're more beautiful
Than most forms of life
Yet you are like death
Creeping into my heart
Stealing my soul
In the silent midnight hours
You are my poverty
Still I am rich
My hope and my depression
To be my companion
Yet the cause of my loneliness
You are an ocean
And I have not yet learned to swim
For I am drowning in you
Possess all that I am
Become pure love
Take me over completely
You are my thoughts
For there is never a moment
When I'm not thinking of you
Let me be near you
Not only for the reasons I cannot say
I do not want you
But I need you
The cure to my sadness
The cause of my misery
My composer
I your symphony
My illness
And the treatment
Still, I make no attempt to escape
You, my protection
An artist and I your canvas
I long to be near you
Distant and far
I cannot hide myself
In the shadow of your perfection
You steal the breath
That I would breathe

Leaving me wanting
To be your desire
Become your obsession
As you have become mine

I Wish

I wish I could write
A song for you
About you
More beautiful
Than you ever heard
I would pour everything
I feel for you into a melody
So sweet and sad
That just to hum the tune
Would make you weep
With joy and sorrow
What words would I use
To capture your heart
Perhaps I would
Make up my own language
So that I might sing
Of your beauty
And you might hear
The pure perfection
Of the very love
I feel for you
But if I were to write
Of all the emotions I feel
That embraces you
In the form of lyrics and melody
In a wondrous harmony
A song I would write for you
Would no longer be a song
But a symphony that would be
Forever played in the contentment
Of your heart

He Remembered

He remembered
The first time he asked me
To be his love
Hiding his face

He remembered
Our first break up
I thought I'd cry
Several oceans

I remembered
Our first slow dance
How I wanted
To stay with him

I remembered
What I longed to forget
For such a very long
Lonely time

He remembered
The first real kiss
The feeling of newness
Our lips

I remembered
When He broke my heart
When I let go
And stopped crying

I asked him
When he first realized
That he was
In love with me

He said
It was the very first time
That he lost me
When I left him

Then I asked

Just when it was
That he stopped

A day late

Is it really over now?
Can I open my swollen eyes?
Do you really not love me anymore?
It's hard for me to realize
That the answers I'm seeking
Are not the ones you'll give
I wish I could make you hold me
Tell me everything is all right
But I know its not
In your heart
You know it too
If I close my eyes again
I'll pretend that you're here
The sad feelings would disappear
Still, when I open them
Things will be as they are
You won't be in love with me anymore
My eyes won't glow
The sun won't shine
The stars won't twinkle
The earth won't spin
If you can walk away
Honestly believing
We're through

November 2004

For so long i waited
wondering about my unanswered questions
Your response was heart chilling
we were better left in the past
take a rusted nail and scratch my name out of Your heart
You bring all of the pain of the things that love is not
the fact that i still care for You only complicates
our situation of endless what ifs and maybes
victims of vindictiveness
You never loved Her but *You sure did love me*
years of silence and avoidance
the pain inflicted by You and She

my joy and my hope ended in an act
and now here You are trying to brand me
asking, begging for another chance
but You took that option away from me
then You gave it to Her
as You sealed our fate between Her legs
so asking what if is futile now
'cause i know me and i know Her
She has claimed You and took what was my hope
i could not graze your lips knowing the truth
the facts would linger in the air and on my mind
don't ever touch me that way that You touched Her
don't think of what You could have had
i would not love You again
be thankful that i'm offering my friendship
seek nothing more than that
You didn't love me enough...
never enough love left to share with me
i won't let you have me
another trophy in Your mind
You'd think, "I did sisters"
i will not let You confuse me
with the never-ending story of our love
You do mean My love, right?
didn't You decide to lay with Her?
weren't You the one that said that i was made for You?
were You thinking about our love
when You were stroking away our future?
I was...
I've thought about it!
especially now that You have decided
that we are going to be together
without My permission
without My consent
I will not, cannot
be with You
burry our past between Her legs
and let Your love for Me wither away
'cause You killed us
three years ago this month

Journal Entry # 6

Dear Journal,
I can say nothing for myself except,
For me, there is no greater sadness
Than to see a grown man fighting tears
And knowing that those tears are for me
He asked for my love and I could only reply
That I had none to give
So he offered to wait until my love was replenished
Then I suggested a friendship
He declined and said that he needed more
But I could not share myself with him
The knowledge of my never ending love
was not enough for him
For me, being aware of his feelings,
Hearing the words grace his lips
Was enough for me
So when he asked me to kiss him
My heart felt heavy and I denied his request
I decided to depart from him with a departure of friends
But he was so eager that he held me tight
And he forced his mouth on mine
My thoughts ran amiss
It's a long road down to hell and I'm sure
That I've got a seat on the train
I pulled away and he hung his head
We broke our embrace
So I walked away forever
I cannot love him in the way that he requires
My sacrifices would be too great
Losing my love, my pride, and my peace
He would have me run mad
To love him only for a day
But I am not yet ready to give my life
Not ready to die

Reflections of a Summer

I adore a man
He has no interest in me
Doesn't understand
Doesn't want to

Doesn't want to like me

I loved a man
He didn't deserve me
Couldn't love me
Couldn't respect me
Couldn't acknowledge my greatness

I had a man worship me
He wanted to die for me
Tried to please me
Tried to seduce me
Tried to correct his wrongs

And I...changed
Somewhere in the mess of things
I gave up
Fell out of love
Misled a weeping man

I might have screwed up

The Past: All grown up

I became afraid
His intentions were to take me
Lust, puberty, and football
The deciding factors
That have made him physically stronger
Than I could ever be
Although I struck him repeatedly
He only laughed
Becoming aroused
As he held me pinned
Between my bed and his erection
I squirmed helplessly
While he delighted in my struggle
The tense grip around my wrists ceased
Saved by being a girl
I was released
No longer pinned by his core
Regained my composure
He undressed to his shorts
We lay in my bed

Exchanging secrets
Offers to touch himself
For my viewing pleasure
I pass up the show
In favor of silent cuddling
It was like he had been taking long walks
Inside of my thoughts
Reading the journal
Locked inside the office of my mind
The words he let trickle
From his mouth into my ears
Made my heart listen
'Cause I had prayed in private
For a man like this
But this one isn't for me
Forgiving is easy
It's the forgetting about my pride
And the past that's the problem

Riddled

It's a dangerous game
Four players
Only one of them knows the truth
There are two being adored
One who was once loved
A woman and three men
The woman has only had one lover
He didn't appreciate her
There is an old, unsettled account
Two will survive the game
But which two?
What will become of the four players
Playing the dangerous game
Of love and obsession
Full of power struggles
Possessive behaviors fueled by deception
When does the game end
When will they be free
We decide today

Reservations

I don't want to do this anymore
It wasn't my intention to cause trouble
Didn't want you to question everything
I just needed to be honest
Had to let you know how I feel
But now...
Our pure intentions are no longer noble
We are no longer void of guilt
Fighting to keep the things they stole from us
I have taken from another
The things I've always considered to me mine
I fought you, ran from you, hurt you
Because I was afraid
I'd love you too much
In giving you my heart, I am trusting that you won't break it
That you will be mindful of your power
That you will understand the sensitivity of this matter

Again

Laying in his arms
Resting after we've made love
I realize the severity of the situation
Tears escape the corners of my eyes
I let him hold me
Listen to the sound of his breathing
The rhythm of his heart
I love this man
I love him for who he is
His good days
His bad days
His depression
His joy
His sensitive insecurities
His masculine confidence
The little boy he was
The man he has become
I love him...
I catch my tears before they scar his skin
While he sleeps holding me
Like we would be that way forever

I love him...
I'm in love with him
Again

It's Like That

Couldn't tell you before
That you were all I wanted
From the moment you uncovered your face
Staring at me from behind your black and red framed glasses
I knew... you were meant for me
I was sprung off your kisses
Though this feeling is not purely sexual
Most times I just want hold you
Love your honesty, warped sense of humor
I'm alive when you look at me
I soar when you acknowledge my presence
When the moment is silent
I love the sound of your rhythm
Kiss your fears away
And make love until
Every part of me is synchronized
With every part of you...
I need you to love me
Love me through my insanities
Love the things about me that you can't understand
Love my eyes and the way they change
Love me for me!
I love your smile
I love your tears, though they are so few
I love your smell and your taste
I love your mind and the way you think
I love you! I love you, I love you
I love you...
And though I am sure you love me too
I need to hear you say it
Want you to explain it so I can understand

Newfound Freedom

Loving you allows me the freedom I've been seeking
Not heavily weighed down with the pressure of commitment
You do not force me to define us
Placing childish titles on what we are

You allow me the freedom to explore
I learn more about you and myself
As individuals and when we join
I understand why there are no words for the love we share
You ignite the spark in me
With cool calm easy going flow
Inspire me to give more
Love harder, stronger, smarter, longer
You cause me to be selfless
Although I do not feel trapped
I remain captivated by you
Teaching me more about love and life
Than I had ever known
You allow me the space to grow
The time to understand my own heart
The feelings I have for you
Patiently waiting for me to be ready for you
Are not forceful without cause
Display restraint until I come to you
Then permit me to give myself
Without taking more
Give me what I can handle
When I feel like I can't take it
Assure me that I can and give me more
I love the way you love to love me
Strong and fearless bearing no restriction
Give your all to me
As I receive you with submission
Grant me permission to love you freely
And I will love you always as I do in this moment

Dear John Letter

I can never quite find the words
To say just what I'm thinking
Or what I'm feeling for that matter
It's hard to tell you that I'm letting go
For the very last time
I'm sorry that I couldn't be all that you wanted
Couldn't give you what you needed for so long
Time has changed your feelings for me
And I'll spare you the details of my heart
The pain that I have carried
I'd ask you if you still care

If I could change our years before
I would not have loved you so much
Or tried so hard to change myself for you
Tears wouldn't have come so often
But I didn't know you were only playing
When I finally told you I loved you
Whole heartedly
The world had stopped turning
You seemed so cold and angry
Then made me feel wrong for being hurt
So I've decided that you should be free
And I shouldn't care
Or love you anymore
So this is as you said it should be
Enjoy the life you've created for yourself...
Without me

So... I Lied

Nameless He

Long strands of onyx
Shade the beauty
Of the windows
To his soul.
Ebony-colored shell
Stretched across
His limbs, so
Perfect that they
Must have been
Created by the
gods of Athens.
Soft lips I
Pray against
Kissing an angel.
His natural grace
And charm make
Him most extraordinary.
He holds favor
With the Greeks
For his form was
Designed by Zeus
And all the beauty
Of his voice
Rest in Aphrodite's arms.
These are only
What the eye can see.
The essence of his
Presence fills the world
With joy and light.
To be held in
The comfort and
Security of his arms
Is to feel your
Entire being
Become elated.
To love him...
Just to love him,
I cannot even
Begin to explain,

For even I am
Left in the shadows of the
Land of the oblivion
When he speaks
Those words,
Yet he says nothing at all.
I am in awe,
Breathless...
Drowning in the
Very thought of him.

I Love You: part 2

I love you
For more reasons
Than my mouth
Will allow me to say
You have filled
My days with
Such unspeakable
Joy and an
Undeniable happiness
Every moment
Is a growing climax
That has no end
Nor would I
Want there to be
It is not life
That I so fear
Only the thought
Of a life
Without you in it
Even though
A day lacking
Your presence
Seems an eternity
The thought of you
Makes long hours
And days pass
Away as if they
Were mere minutes
Time is escaped me
Only when I am
In your arms

Hold me

Broken

I am very much afraid
That you will find another
To replace me in your heart
Although not intentionally
Love takes the place of choice
Whereby free-will is nonexistent
She is taken with you
Intertwining your name with hers
Carving it anywhere that she can
Once I thought you were my new world
The way to start over
My land of dreams
Awakened by the sight of her and you
Walking closely together
My heart sank lower than hell depths
Just now, in this moment
You want nothing more that her
She something more with you
And I nothing but to be with you
Don't be a stranger

No Idea

I always thought
We would be different
That we would have
Something to transcend time
Now I'm not so sure
About my hopes
There is nothing I fear
More than losing you
Or realizing that we
Are no longer
Or never were
This was unexpected
My feelings for you
Never thought I would
Care for you so much
Yet I'm wondering
If this time was spent in vain

Perhaps you feel not a thing
I am but your leisure activity
It hurts
Just the thought brings me to tears
You don't know
How this is killing me
You have no idea

Drowning Me

I cried inside of myself
A river so vast and deep
That it became the ocean
And drowned my heart

I am forever in love
With you for every second
Of every day
For the rest of my life

I smile for you
Only to hide the tears
Of immense love
Unstoppable emotion

I don't want to let go
It's much too hard
Can't let you walk away
Because you do love me

I won't cry in front of you
Won't cry for the world to see
I'm crying inside of myself
Slowly drowning me

Midday Phone Calls

There are times when I am sure
That I don't deserve you
Nights when I lay awake
In your arms I am
Praying that God let you stay
Midday phone calls

You say "I love you"
The call is for just that purpose
Gladly I give myself, my love
I belong to you by choice
With firm conviction
I stand by you
Believing in our love and in us
I am fortunate to know you
And if I could hold you
For the rest of my days
Contentment would be an understatement
God made me obedient and understanding
I love you without boundaries
Without end

Don't Blame Me

Don't blame me if I
Can't let you go
As swiftly as you'd like
Its only hard 'cause
You still are so many
Things that I need and
The things that I wanted
We're just friends now
But in my heart…
It just won't accept
That we are no longer
I'm trying hard,
Not to stop caring, but
To be your friend
So that I don't lose you
Completely
Even though my wishful thinking
Is just that, I wonder
What am I doing here
And why aren't we together?
If you want to be free
I know I can't make you stay
Just wish that things were different

Open Arms

When it's over
I hope that it would have all been worth it
We'll hug, maybe a kiss
And only one word... goodbye
I loved you
Like no one has ever loved another
I know that it really is over
But I'm not giving up
I just won't chase you
You'll come home when you're ready
And I'll be here
With open arms

Care Much Lately

There are days when I miss you
More than the other days
I still hurt inside
When I think of letting you go
Part of me wants you back
The other part of me knows better
Tells me that I'm too good for you
It's the truth, and we know it
I wanted to love you forever
But you didn't trust me to do that
Something inside of me ceased to exist
Questions: I want to know about everything
You don't have the answers
Neither do I
We struggle to maintain civility
Though bitter and hurt
Making ill attempts at sustaining friendship
When we both know that you don't deserve that
So why am I still trying when it's clear
That you couldn't care less

Sleepless

I kick you into the dark corner in my mind
Trying to forget about all that has been
It doesn't help
Just keep thinking about the way you kiss

How you are so gentle when I'm in your arms
You seem so perfect
Yet I know that you are not
I'll not treat you unkind
I must admit, if not to you, then only to myself
That I am bitter and full of anger
The nights are like restless hours
Of useless hoping and sleepless dreams
I'd ask if you still care for me
The answer, I'm sure, would shatter me
I'd be broken glass
I could be sad, but I won't show it
Tell my secrets to the Lord above
To blank pages in a book
I close my eyes
Sleepless

Time

Often times when I
Am with you I
Don't think that
There are enough hours
In the day for me
To spend with you
People see us and
Smile in admiration
Our joy shines
Through every
Darkness, you offer
Such great gifts
That I feel so
Unworthy to
Be in your life
If I could save
Every moment
Of everyday that
I have spent with you
I would take them
And relive every second
In my old age
For nothing can compare
To the time I have...
The time we have spent...

All the beauty
That I see
When I am with you

Where are you

I'm seeing the daytime reflection
Of a night spent with you
Overlooking the lake
But you're not here
Watching the harbor
The sunlight finds you missing
We only see each other in the shadows
Still the rusted metal sheet reminds me
Of the warmth of your body
Your body my anchor
I want to hold you down until you want...
To stay in the light
So you can see the sun kiss my eyes
Ignite the wick that imitates a hazel hue
You scamper off into the darkness
Swing swinging on my emotions
Because at night you'll hold my hand
At the lake
In night's reflection of the day
You're nowhere to be found

Young and Stupid

This feeling that I have
I wouldn't trade it
For all the world

There are moments
Of pure joy and happiness
That fill me completely

There are seconds
Of intense feelings
Enough to push me over the edge

I feel immense pain
A sadness so deep
Tears won't flow

I feel as if my entire existence
Is being crushed
And put back together again

If I ever stopped feeling
This way I would
Be empty and lifeless

Being so desperate
To be in his presence
Just to see him

Should I ever let this feeling go
I would be
Nothing at all

I know that to feel pure joy
I must feel total desperation
At the same time

If I don't have this feeling
I have nothing
I've met my end

All I can do is give all of me
Wait for him to love me
Decide that he wants me

Even though my love
May never feel the same for me
I love him anyway… desperately

The boy who wrote me Poetry

The boy who wrote me poetry
Wrote that I was a goddess
Wrote that I was beautiful
Wrote the beauty of my eyes
Wrote that he would love me forever
And he meant it

The boy who wrote me poetry
Wrote about the grace of my touch

Wrote about the way I glide
Wrote about being in my presence
And he was honest

The boy who wrote me poetry
Wrote about his sleepless nights
Wrote about my golden skin
Wrote about my dark hair
And he called it a song

The boy who wrote me poetry
Wrote two poems for me
Wrote about his thoughts of me
Wrote about his longing
Wrote about wanting me
Wrote things that made me cry
Wrote things that made me write back
And he made me immortal

Prophesy

Last night I cried myself to sleep
Images played in my subconscious
We were over and you were pleased
In the back of my mind
I always thought you didn't care
You left me and never looked back
Tried to hide you dirt-covered hands
You scrubbed them until you thought they were clean
But the dirt remained under your fingernails
You were wrong about us
Sadly I was right
My mind whispers to me harsh words
Like you never loved me at all
Now the tears bleed through my pillow
And I awake the same way I fell
Although only a dream
I know that it's the truth
Just waiting to break into daylight

Truth

In the confines
Of your arms
I found freedom
And let my body
Tell you secrets
My eyes told
You everything
Just by their colors
Still you question
What is truth?
Truth is:
Me never wanting
To say goodnight,
Every embrace
That I gave to you,
Tender kisses pressed
Into my hands,
Crying at the thought
Of losing you,
Watching you sleep/
To know that we
Are about to be
No longer
Is more than I can take/
The fact that you could
End it all
So quickly;
Would you give
It a second thought
Or make it nothing
More than a suppressed memory?
I love you
And that's the truth/
I'm strong enough
To admit that
I don't know everything...
That I don't know
How it's going to be
When you confess
That you want out
How I'm going to feel
When I realize

That I may have
Imagined you returning
My affections and being
Sensitive to my charms
That I was
In love...
Alone/
Maybe you did
Care abut "us"
But then again
I thought that you knew
Me better than you did
And I never really
Knew you at all
Not like that
Because I thought
That you were Love
'Cause I was Faith and
Our relationship was Hope/
But that was
And still is
Just a Dream
That I was dreaming/
For you it was
A nightmare
From which
You couldn't awake
No escape/
I was captured
By make-believe
And hurt by reality/
So it's your decision
To stay or to leave
Now I'm just waiting
For you to break
My heart
Once more/
I still love you
And that
Is the God's honest
Truth

One Month

It's been one month
One whole month
The hardest part is the wanting
If I could control the urge
To kiss you
The wanting to be in your arms
The security of belonging to you
Then I'm sure that I'd be okay
But for you the hardest part
Is not knowing what the future holds
So knowing just who holds it
Gives me some comfort
And offers you none
Even if it's over for good
I'm glad that you were
My first love and lover
Such a formidable one at that
Maybe someday you'll surprise me
With a platinum band
Decorated with a posted sapphire surrounded by diamonds
Armed with love and conviction
Knowing that you deserve me
To ask a question
Perhaps my answer would be pleasant
Then again, I can't work on you
I can only work on me...
Too emotionally fucked up to move on just yet
Still crying myself to sleep some nights
Good days, bad days
Too unstable to eat at times
But it's been one month
And I am still surviving
As your friend

Make it Simple

I miss...
Sipping honey form your lips
In the moments when
We knew what love was
The days when I only
Wanted your company

And didn't need to feel you
The simple days
Private endeavors meant to seal love
Lead to our downfall
I felt closest to you
While convulsed in madness
And you took my only joy
Shared it with another
Brought it back to me damaged
I made you immortally love
To have you fill me with insecurity
Unable to love me through it
Like I needed you to
And still I miss
Kissing you...in simple terms

Your Request

Last night
 You gently restated your request
"Please still love me"
My promise was made long
Before you ever asked for it
Love is not always by choice
But when love takes precedence
Reason is but a far off concept
We do not control
Matters of the heart
Yet we so desperately try
If it is in our hearts
To be joined then all else
Is nothing more than a test
For destiny should find me
Asleep in your arms
I dare not stray!
The reward will be
All the more sweet
After the triumph
I will love you until
Everything on earth is
No longer in existence
And still more after that
You shall not escape me
Your request is granted

Taunts from Truth

Truth is such an intricate thing
There's nothing like it
After you've waited months
Nothing compares to hearing one's love
Disclose the secrets kept inside
Hearing the truth from a friend
Just doesn't compare
Takes away its luster
But when it's dreamt about
It's going to be the defining moment
Who can make it and who can't
Deep inside, I knew the truth
I just needed to hear the man I loved say it
I wouldn't believe it if he didn't say it
The thing that hurt wasn't that I had found out
But Truth seeks to be known
She needs to be seen and heard
Listening to Damien Rice's "O"
As my world fell to nothing
He sang the lyrics
Appropriate for the occasion
And that is the sad thing about knowing the truth
Knowing doesn't change the truth
It only makes the perception of it different
The truth gave me some peace
Put upon me some burdens
And revealed to me…
I will always love the man who told me the truth
I would rather know the truth
Than to be taunted by it

The Cut

The cut was deep
Much deeper than I had originally thought
It was deep enough
So that my tourniquet could not stop the bleeding
The cut was complex
And since there was no way
To properly dress the wound
The infection set in
Spread through my circulatory system

Flooding me as the dam of sanity burst
Resulting in illness
Regurgitating the love that I had ingested
Continued to be malnourished
On sugar-sprinkled lies
Cup-cake deception topped with
Imitation cherry kisses
The cut has left me weak
Stumbling around like a lush
I gave up on life again
Tried to fight off the disease
But it was much too late
The cut of life had seriously wounded me
Infection of love killing me slowly
And a malnourished relationship
Finished me off

Uncertainty

I'm not sure if I still love you
You're only with me because you pity me
Scared that I won't make it without you
I'm much stronger than you give me credit for
I think the last time you broke my heart did it
You had broken it twice before
But now I've really had enough
Tired of purchasing your 'favors'
You actually think that I would sabotage my future behind you
I'm smarter than that
DAMN!!
I don't even look at you the same
You rarely pique my curiosity anymore
You lack ambition
A crime you once accused me of
Too selfish to make me your number one
God goes without saying 'cause He is everything to me
Still you project your insecurities on me
It's you who won't make it without me
You once told me that you loved me
But if you had to, you would walk away
And never think about me again
Maybe you should collect on that promise
You would die if I didn't love you!
I know it and you do too

So why don't you love me the way that you should?
Why don't you match me
Love me through my insanities?
When am I going to be your everything?
You are not worthy!
You're not, you're not, you're not!
And by the time that you convert
To something remotely resembling
The type of man that I deserve
I'll have already moved on
Then what?
I'm not sure if I still love you
Here is your chance to decide:
Are you going to love me the way that I've loved you?
Are you going to correct your mistakes?
Can you earn the right to have me?
Or am I asking too much of you?

Fallout

September 2, 2005
Dear Journal,
I've come to the ultimate
Realization of hurt
He touched me and there was nothing...
I was completely void of want
And for the first time in years
I wasn't in love
It hurt not to want him
To be missing that part of me
That had been ever present
I became someone I didn't like
Did things just for him
It hurts not to love him the same
When there was a time
That I wanted to love him forever
But now, there's nothing
Just the awkward feelings
Like being in the arms of a stranger
He isn't the boy that I once loved
Nor the man that I thought he'd be
Only the drunken shadow
Of the 16-year-old boy I knew
I don't think I'm in love with him...

This new creature...
Anymore

Moments of Wretchedness

Cell phone slipped
Fingers clenched
I exhale
Feel my body react
To the sound of the phone
Embrace the tiled floor
And just as sure as I knew
That I was breathing,
I knew that he would come for me
Quickly regain composure
Pick my phone up off of the floor
And attempt to salvage my sanity
I return to the front end
To see him enter through the automatic door
Close behind his mother
He knows I see him
With the expression of
"What the fuck do you want?"
Clear upon my face,
I wait for him to approach
Just as I knew he would
His mother initiates conversation
I don't acknowledge him
He speaks...
I feel sick
Upon looking him in the face
How dare he speak to me!
This new being
That I once loved the shadow of
He is not that boy
This wounded man standing before me
His eyes begging for something
That I once gave him
But will not give again...
He's sorry, all over his face
He walks away
As I fight angry tears and fatigue
I can't breathe
I hate him for hurting me

Wounding me to the point of infection
And I hate him for loving me as he dies
'Cause the lack of me in his life
Is killing him
I hate him for not realizing sooner
That I am all he would ever need
For not wanting me enough to change
And for forcing me to see him
Against my will
I hate him for trying
When it's far too late...
To fix us...
Just go away
Leave me alone
I'm over him
But he's not over hurting me
He never will be

Thoughts on 21

Three years ago
I had planned this day
He and I would celebrate
By getting piss drunk
And making love
Until we passed out
He would have a good job
Waiting for him
After we graduated from college
So in love
That all would be envious
My family anxious in the house
Like him
Waiting for tomorrow
So he could ask me
To make him complete
In the eyes of God
On the day that he
First confessed his love
My joy would fill depths
Of every thought of love
I ever had for him
But those plans are wasted hopes
On a life and love that I imagined

As I look back at 18
With thoughts on 21

Finally Breathing

When I first looked into your eyes
There was nothing to be done
My heart stopped and the moment
Almost passed me by
Now as the days grow in number
I wish it had
Was it worth all the trouble in the first place
I wonder if our hello was better
Than our goodbye
At the beginning I held my breath
And now, I'm exhaling you out

Wanting: The Payback of Scorn

I want to belong to you
Allow you to break me down inside
And build me back up
I long to be within your possession
Be your obsession
The drug that you can't give up
The reason you won't back away
I want to be yours
Be your addiction
Comfort, solace, seduction
Companion, conviction
I want you to feel entitled to me
Believe that you are worthy
Understand that you must fight
That you will know long suffering
Experience soul saving sacrifice
I want to be your high
The quick fix you need to make it through life
The peaceful calm/come down
Pain that overtakes you
The cure for every heartache
The one thing that will break you
Make you, mold you, hold you
Keep you from the dangers of self
I want to be your sanity

That thing that makes you cry
Decides if you die or live
I want to give you love
Make you sing, dance, weep with joy
Be your lover, quench your thirst
Satisfy your desires
Be your drive, pride, pleasure
Be the lyrics to your song
Cause the right to seem such
Your struggle to get clean
Good enough to cause wrong
The light in your dark corner
Your religion, weakness, strength
Denial, redemption, escape
Be the reason you wake
The dream that makes you long for sleep
A collision of concepts that you don't understand
The air that you breathe
A beat in your heart
The words you can't speak
The love that you lost
I want to be your **_EVERYTHING!_**
I've earned it
I deserve it
But you leave me with nothing
My sweet hurt
Deliciously bitter taste dissolves
Fades into the remembrance of flavor
I am your nothing...
And that is all you'll ever have

Three-way Split

The "us" died a while ago
I buried a piece of me with it
The part of me that I felt you made come alive
Thought that you gave me life
But you were killing me
Not alive at all but dying rather quickly
She was the naïve in me
The foolish love of confined commitment
Love as the construct of captivity
Is not love at all
But control...

A new beast to battle
Corrupted love/ trust with power
Of playing the roles of dominant and submissive
The you of "us" was clever
And I was tricked and trapped
Unable to see that I was no longer myself
I aimed to be your wants
Detouring from who I should have been
I am the person that I was on my way to being
You don't know me and therefore cannot love me
I've taken off the "you make everything so beautiful" glasses
I see you for who you are
Not the person I imagined you to be
You are not my love/ life
You are something else
One third of "us"
You are the control
She was the naïve
And I am finally free

The Seduction of Eve

Tear blurred
Nearly swollen shut eyes
Sleep deprived
I cried for weeks
Over the weakness
In giving you my heart
All leading to the derivations
Of misplaced affections
Disappointed hopes
Don't want you back
But can't believe you're over me
Ready to pledge your heart
Give your name
To her...
You're faithful
A provider
Granter of desires
For her!!!
Why not for me?
Was I not everything a woman should strive to be?
Sweet, giving
Obedient, with a fire

That you tried to smother
To quiet your own insecurities
I GAVE UP EVERYTHING FOR YOU!
Just to watch you
Pour it into her little olive hand
In debt, emotionally scarred
Overrun with self doubt
Curious as to what the hell is wrong with me
That you didn't see fit
To love me
Return to me what I offered you
Which you took so gladly
I threw my pearls to a pig
And you did trample them
Turning around to rip me apart
But you let her be whole...
She's your good-morning kiss
The tear on your pillow at night
And I...
Am nothing more than a faint whisper
From a past you left
Long forgotten
Left and discarded
Like partially eaten fruit
In the sun
Overtaken by maggots
With the seeds doomed to die
On a table with no hope of a wind
To scatter them to fertile soil...
What's so wrong with me?
Nothing...
I just experienced the seduction of Eve
I was deceived
And you were the serpent

Journey into Green

First time seeing

He doesn't know it
But I relive the first time
That I saw him in my mind
He was standing in line
In a bookstore
I was in the stairwell
I saw him and was frozen
The memory plays back
In slow motion
I could do nothing but watch him
Clear green eyes
Honey colored skin
Easy pink lips…
I thought, how gorgeous?
About six two
Large frame but nicely built
Assembled well
I knew that I wanted to know him
But I was too weak
Too shy to go up and speak
So I only watched
As he exited the store
And disappeared
Into the opposing stairwell
I ran down the second flight
But not down the last
I stayed hidden
To watch him float by

Just Thinking

I've played with the idea of us
When you come near
My heart palpitates
And my mind runs wild
With thoughts of you and I
It's too much at times
So I wonder how I would react
If you touched my hand

If you pressed your body against mine
In an embrace
I think of all the ways
I could love you like a man
Because you are one, truly
Love and express it on levels
Of intimacy with you
I could experience your levels of love
Maybe add a new one
Becoming more intense
Than the ones before
But you've never felt
The way that my love could drown you
Its currents are not defeated
But I wouldn't let it take you under
I'm pleased with your individuality
The idea is much to immaculate
To be said aloud
So I whisper the thoughts
Into my subconscious mind

Are You Happy, Beautiful?

There's a happiness that I wanted
For you, only for you
But I think that you've felt it before
Maybe in another life
Because your smile is one of joy
Beauty and serenity
Are you happy, Beautiful?
Are you really happy?
In my dreams we're always talking
And you always say something profound
Or something that I hadn't thought of
Always something hiding behind your eyes
They say what your smile doesn't
So I wonder if that's the profound thing
That you say in my dreams
Because I can never remember what you said
I only know that when I awake
The dream dissolves and my heart is light
Maybe I'll tell you the truth
Then again I don't think you need to hear it
And I don't think that you'd really care to either

At another time perhaps
Again I'll ask
Are you happy, Beautiful?
Are you really happy?
I don't think that you are
And I'm sure that you don't care
You don't know just how far I'd go
How much I could take
That I wouldn't give up
Until I could make you--
Until you wanted to--
Smile at me
Smile for me
Just smile

Secret Infatuation

We're just too far apart
I'm not sure of your feelings
One second you are warm and responsive
The next, you seem cold and distant
I want you more, I'm sure
Than any of the others
My need is much greater
And my appreciation
Would exceed theirs by miles
And like a Catholic, I'm confessing
But with a pencil, and this paper
Is my priest
My idealization of you is my sin
So I confess but do not ask forgiveness
I'm not sorry for my desire
Yet you! You are leading me on
Constantly letting me down
Still I want to surround you
Want to be near you 99.9% of the day
The 0.1% that is not spent wanting
Is when I am in your company
But that is not enough
Need to be with you in comfort
In silence
In truth
This has transgressed want
Become basic necessity

So I'm thinking that I'm crazy
'Cause you've said nothing
To indicate that you feel anything
Remotely close to my manifestations
But I need you to
And wish that you did

First Hit

I am standing on the edge of sanity
Being taunted by the truth to jump
I don't want to plunge into the unknown
But lust pushes me beyond my limits
I fall quickly into the danger zone
There is no salvation
As I embrace the empty air and silence
I swing at foolish hopes with empty hands
There is only me sinking into the darkness
No one understands and they couldn't help me anyway
I'm not sure that I want to be saved
'Cause I like the mystery
The danger of it all
Pulling me in deeper
Until there is no chance of an escape
Trapped in you with desire
I want so much more
But I'm taking all that you'll give me
I've never been this scared
This far away from my sanity
And the person that I thought I was
I'm afraid of what's going to happen
When you touch me again
Will I give in?
Am I strong enough to handle it?
Will this be the last time?
I'm praying that the fire in you
Doesn't consume me entirely
What will be left of me
After I give you what I've allowed you to take?
I'm not sure what you want
But it's yours for the asking
Just grant me a moment of peace
A sip from his mouth
That sweet release that he promised me

As I became intoxicated with his aroma
And high off his touches
Drunk on his mouth and the words that he spoke
My body becomes inflamed
There is no turning back from this point
And I want nothing more
Than to feel him spreading through me
Poison in my veins
I've sold my soul
Trying to get a hit of you

Music Junkie

My drug of choice...
Musical fixes
And lyrical highs
Poetry moving
I love the way
The bass disturbs my heartbeat
All that's left
Is the vibrating in my chest and throat
It possesses me completely
So I give in and let the beat
Flow into me
Wash over me
I accept it with ease
Taking it all into me
Until I am entirely filled
With all that is music...
All that is beauty...
All that is...
This man

Taking a Serious Interest

I sit and stare out the window
Hoping that you'll walk by
So I can look at you
And I admire you in the open
So that everyone can see
The man passing the little girl
The foolishness in me
I'm begging you to touch me
While I'm backing away

I was warned about you
Told that I couldn't do without you
But you don't even notice me
I'm crying your name
Into the pillows
When I touch myself
There is no doubt in my mind
That you're what my life is missing
On the days when I am lonely
Confronted by the very nature
Of the tension rising between your legs
And the softening between mine
I want to push you
To the way that I feel when I know
That you should be deeper
That you should be kissing me
But you won't allow us to venture
Down that path
And rightfully you should be afraid
I don't know what I'd do
When I am with you

The Words

I want so much more
But I can't find the words on my own
Maybe I would find them in your bed
With my face pressed into the pillows
Are the words smothered between our embraces?
Are they gathered in the space where my lips
 lightly brush your neck?
Did I lose them in your smile
Or perhaps I left them lingering
In the air with the smell of your cologne?
Perhaps they were drowned out
by the deep chords of your voice
I know where the words are,
They are caught in my throat when I try to say them to you
They are locked behind my smile when I see you
Involuntarily pouring out of my eyes in semi-sweet tears
I wasn't speaking until I whispered your full name
Not being clever until I thought of ways to talk to you
Couldn't see until I caught a glimpse of you
Never inflamed until

You touched me
I have the words...
They just can't be said

Things That I Can't Have

I find myself
Throbbing at the thought of you
I imagine you caressing my body
My hands begin to move
Over my special places
They linger in the spots
That needs the most attention
And my hands
Become your hands
And our hands begin
The journey of exploring
Me more deeply
I arch and rise
At the entrance of fingers
Into my candy store
We've got to use both hands
To make sure that we have multiple
Explosions and earth shaking moments
I shudder and shake
Enfold you gently all around
Then my thoughts leave
Your hands to focus
On the other parts of you
That I am anxious to explore
Exploring all the parts of me
And we test our theories
About pleasure and pressure
We reach the climax
Of soundless numbness
With pulsing vibrations
Now all that remains
Is me with thoughts of you
Lingering in the air
A silent reverie
I crave more
Need to feed the addiction
Or risk the withdrawals
But you're a drug

That I've yet to take
And already I'm a fiend
So my imagination
Runs wild once more
I receive you with
Soothing, wet warmth
Until you're all the way inside
Move in and out
Up and down
Until my walls collapse
Along with my mind
And I'm so tired
From the mental
Teasing the physical
That I let the contracting
Of the candy store's walls
Put me to sleep
So that I can dream
About what you might
Actually feel like
But still the dream
Is not enough
Not vividly fulfilling
I seek the real thing
Wanting things that I don't need
Needing things that I shouldn't want
Want and need things that I can't have

Why Me

I am not crazy
Though in my mind
I think that I must be
I miss the subtle things
The way that he grinds his teeth when angry
How he smiles softly at private thoughts
The way he fumbles over words
When he looks at me…
Why me

The Assassin

He makes the world stop
Provokes me to sing
Arouses my creativity
With just a look...
His words inspire lustful thoughts
Hugs move me to insanity
Kisses reduce me to panic
I lose my breath
And fight the urge to cry
He is killing me
I am letting him
Dying with every passing day
Lustful word, sweet smile
Tight embrace, thoughtful compliment
Giggle, gaze, scent, song
Touch, lack of kiss
Sway, back arch, body bend
Yearning, lonely moment...
This assassin
Murdering me with his seduction
Is fully aware
But lacking concern

Faker

Who is this imposter?
He pretended for so long
That he convinced himself
I was sure that I had seen
The real version of the man
Want of him left me yearning
Exacerbated my emotions
He led me to believe
That he was capable
Of loving a woman like me
I knew that I would never have him
But still I tried for his affections
An imitation of the type of man
I thought he was
So deceiving

With his sensual talks of
Oral pleasures
He is an actor
Seasoned from the lies he lived
Still, I want to know him... really
And love him as a friend

Rain Dance

As the rain fell upon him
It made music
I listened with soft ears
And watched him with wanting eyes
The rain pierced his clothing
Sliding across his skin
Much in the fashion that I desired to
His movements like synchronized dance
I should join him
But the show is enthralling
The rain rolled down his body
As he continued along his walk
Soaked clothes clinging to his flesh
I envy his shirt more than I envy the rain

Do you ever dream of me?

I dream of you quite often.
Mostly on the weekends,
Sometimes during the week.
I'm not sure why
But you stay on my mind.
I've frequently wondered
What would happen
If you heard my confessions,
If I told you that I've dreamt
Of you every weekend since August,
If I told you how I anticipate
Seeing you and how I long
To taste your mouth, your kiss?
Would you think me foolish?
Would you laugh at me?
I know that I can't
Look you in the face for too long.
I'm sure that I would

Stare at you and become
Unable to look away.
You seem so unaware
But I know that you know,
That you aren't oblivious,
Yet you never respond
To the subtle hints
Or to the bold statements.
You've completely dismissed
The thought, the very idea
That I would have...
That I could be—
Something that you desired,
Maybe needed even.
Do you ever dream of me?

Brief Exchange

I could cry
He knows only the surface
Of my wanting
My trying to make him want me
But he didn't...
No... wouldn't
Couldn't get past being his acquaintance
Reduced to a groupie
A member of his ever-growing fan club
I want to stop wanting him
Deny his touches
Become void of my natural self
When in his presence
I am unanimated
Steady making attempts to escape
His gaze
Am caught in his eyes
He is searching me
I deny him the pleasure of my thoughts
Block him from looking into me
He is motionless
I move away
Hoping that I didn't shatter
We disperse in separate directions
I watch him walk away
Eyes long to purge

                    Brain tells eyes "request denied"
                          Tears reside into ducts
                                I am not crying
                                   But I could

Playful Words

                              In my imagination
                            I've heard those words
                                 A thousand times
                          But never passing your lips
                              So today you say them
                         And in a manner so playful
                     Don't tease me with those words
                         'Cause when you say them
                         I feel a calm and a peace
                       With heart stopping excitement
                        And elation all rolled into one
                              When you touch me
                           Jolts pass through my body
                    So much so that I feel I can't take it
                             Yet I do just to feel you
                             Touching me once more
                                  This is endless
                    Because you say those words in jest
                       And I yearn to hear them in truth

To Dream a Dream

Something special about dreams
My dreams speak to me
Prepare me for certain eventualities
But my dreams of him...
Every time that I decide
To put him out of heavy rotation
In the cycle of my thoughts
I dream about him
Our friendship is one-sided
He doesn't even know much about me
It was just something different
Something so enticing about him
That the first time I saw him
I knew that I wanted to know him
His efforts are minimal

The truth as I see it is quite simple
He isn't worthy of my time
Nor of my friendship
So why do I keep having these dreams
Of he and I being together?
Perhaps he is the dream
And I am not awake

Dream of a Dream

I attempt to blotch him from memory
Clear the corners of my mind
Close my eyes and rest my thoughts
He is still there
Lingering somewhere in the subconscious
I had the dream about dreaming about him
Daydreams manifest to nightmares
Tortured and tormented
Struggling to free myself from sleep
From the thoughts of him
I long to purge him from me
But I have inconveniently allowed him
To infiltrate my core
I've taken him in
And am unable to retract the dream
Once in the dream about a dream am trapped
Suffering through fictitious actions
Of he and I
Know better than to indulge
Yet, I can't get out
Can't stop the dream I'm dreaming
So I just sleep
Impossible to awake to a reality
That is far less pleasing than the dream
Still a reality that I am seeking nonetheless
Please... make it go away
Make it stop
Let me rest
I beg him please...
As he does nothing

The Reaction of my Actions (Unexpected cont.)

I am waiting
Remembering the taste of perfection
The taste of love
Savoring every sweet moment
Of touching and tasting greatness
The sensation of a gentle bite and tug
Tongue sliding past lips
Pressed together
The gentle current
Urgently passing through me
Moving me to tears
I have never felt that way
Never experienced such a moment
I have yet to recover
So I am waiting
Praying that the feeling return
But it doesn't
Nothing seems to compare
To his kiss
Unexpected

Lucid

I dreamed him...
For there was no logical explanation of the sensations
He provoked in me
At the feel of his touch
My body would respond with heat
His embrace a haven of hell flames
But a haven at least
Struggle to convince him of my worthiness
He semi-aware of his powers
We interact and make exchanges
Viewed as deep by outside observers
They lack the true understanding of us
As I am confused on him as well
Became unable to distinguish dream from lucid
So I conclude that the entire...
It was all a dream
Every event, poem, moment, spoken word,
Allowed me to fall

Into the sweet sad solitude of my dreams
Disillusioned about this love
Yet I did love him
Still he and I...
We only exist in my dreams

Wake Me

I dreamed him again
Though I strive to suppress
My latent desires
The dreams repeat the theme
That I still want him
Realizing that I know nothing
In all actuality
I love the man I perceive him to be
To deny that emotion
Would be to lie to myself
So while I know that he is unaware
That he is oblivious to my affections
I'll offer him my friendship
In hopes that the man he truly is
Will dismiss my overwhelming perception of him
That he will allow me to know him
Permit me the pleasure of his presence
Dispel my foolish notions of love
With clear and present friendship
So that my love for him will not fade
But grow and become more warranted
There the bond be forged by companionship
And though I may have been disillusioned
Foolish, naïve enough to fall in love
I welcome the friendship
Not of the man I perceived him to be
Not the he that I dream of
The he that he is in reality

Nighttime Ritual

He is the place where my heart leads me
When my mind is at rest
When I am alone with my thoughts
In the quiet darkness
Private prayers

My mind is content to rest
On thoughts of he and I
A fantasy...
Pretend love and elaborate affair
I say nothing
As the thoughts manifest into words
Telling my secrets to the shadows
And for a moment
He is there
Hearing every wish
Granting my desires
While whispering words that will fade
When sunlight breaks the trance
Of this sweet sleep solitude
I rest in the arms of thoughts of him
Until daybreak singe the softness of the moment
He no longer there
My mind in disarray
I awake and only seeking a place
To bury my face and recapture peace
But he is gone...
So there is no rest for me
Though all I crave is him
The he in "us" and my sweet sleep

Unintentionally Misled

I may have imagined you
Or rather perfected you in my mind
Magnified your qualities
Until I convinced myself
That you were all that I needed
But I wanted mostly your physical
Tricked myself into loving you
One-sided friendship
You, the inactive party
Rejection teach me about beauty
I hear sound so differently
Feel things on levels that you can't comprehend
Be honest, you don't want anything
To do with me, do you?
I made the mistake
Of thinking...
You don't understand me

That's why we're not friends
I'm not desirable to you
Don't fit into your perception
Of femininity and definition of sexy
You don't know anything...
About me

His Eyes

When I look into his eyes
I want to run away from home
Not my physical, literal home
He having the keys to my heart/ home
I am left wanting to flee
To escape his piercing gaze
I move to view my heart...
The place where he enters and exits so freely
I am no longer sane
His eyes haunt my memories
In his eyes I am lost
A long, long way away from home
With no hope of direction
He has the power
Makes use of my intentions for him
Embrace me in full body contact
I am unable to keep still
Be still my heart/home
In which he stole so cleverly
Unknowing that my heart
Is his possession
And I am homeless
Wandering in the vast green desert of his eyes
I am lost
Praying that he will find me
Invite me into his heart/home
To live and be loved
As he holds the keys...
To me
I am only looking
Into his eyes

King Lyrical

He is unaware
I fall into his world
Where he is the king
The rest his loyal servants
I being the most naïve
Hoping that he'll allow
My presence in his palace
Wishing to please him
Waiting to be chosen
Like many others
Praying to be bedded
But I am different
Loving my master/captor
While the others fear him
I hold him in reverence
Longing to pursue his mouth
Explore his body
Still in his eyes
I am no more special than the others
They want his prestige
The power of his kingdom
The privilege of his seed
My sole interest
Is to love him
To give him everything
He doesn't understand
I'm not asking for is hand
Just the chance to be with him
Only once
To love him the way he deserves
Then I'll leave his world
If that's what he wants

Lies: Distorted Truths

Lies are the truths
We convince ourselves to believe
I wish that I had a garden
To rip apart
To bury the feelings
I've tried to forget
Ignore and deny

But won't go away
I tell myself that he
Is nothing more than a conquest
A goal to be reached and surpassed
I know better
He pierced me
Penetrated the surface
Embedded himself into my core
He has changed me
And I struggle with reality
The truth is that
I don't need him
I'm not in love with him
This is just a phase
It's the truth that I force me to believe
That's my lie

For Unlawful Carnal Knowledge

He knew...
From the moment I opened my mouth
Read line 1 of my poem
He knew/ I wrote for him
He knew that the moments
Intense and complex
Lustful and hushed
Would no doubt
Lead me to certain levels of inspiration
Feeling him so good
I feel me literally
Wanting more than his mouth
Which once originally was thought to be enough
He knew that I would seek more
But denied my request
Refusing to explain
Ignoring questions unasked
Knowing that I wanted answers
He knew
I wanted the truth
For him to be man enough
To admit that I scare him
That he's afraid to know me
From fear of wanting something more
And I...

                              Am terrified
              From having touched perfection
                 To be denied another touch
                    Steal, bite, lick, suck
                Tongue touch, lips press kiss
                      I didn't ask for more
             Yet he knew I wanted something
                     He knew what I wanted
                            But I didn't
                For unlawful carnal knowledge

Fool

In this moment
I do love you
Knowing that this
Is wrong clouds
Only my mind
For still in my heart
Lies the truth
Here in the dark
It is the only
Crime that I
Have committed
Forgive me for
Confessing so quickly
But by having
Purged my heart
I'll no longer suffer
And if fate should
Grant me such a deed
You could pledge
Your unfailing devotion
Love seems too much
To ask of this...
Devotion is all that
You will part with
When I so desire
Only your heart
And its love
Still I am your slave
Only a fool

Knowing is Half the Battle

If I could understand this
Perhaps I could control it
You display restraint
While I spiral into panic
I'm in love with you
Though you are very unaware of it
Seemingly so much so
That I question if you notice me at all
When the world is silent
Do you ever think of me?
Do you long for the pleasure of my company?
Do you notice when I'm not there?
Do you ever miss me?
Just a little?
I'm sure I know the answers...
Only wanted to hear you say it
If not for the sake of being honest
Say it to ease my wondering mind
Tell me that I imagined you
Tell me you want me to stop...
If you wanted me to lie, I could
I could tell you that I don't love you
That I never think about you
That you didn't affect me in any way at all
I could do anything for you
Just help me to understand
Why don't you want me
Why don't you need me
And tell me why I love you
Because if I could understand us
Then I could control me

Complacent Fixation

Uncomfortably content
A feeling that worries me
I started to like you
Really like you and all of the things that you stand for
Representing a real man
My desire is your friendship
I'm troubled by the fact
I could love you

You could hurt me
The need for you to want me,
Love me
Is sustained by our embraces
I want to say everything
Get it all down on paper
The thought of how my situation
Is so unfair
There's a man that I gave the world
He squandered his time in my Eden
Another is ready to grant me the desires of my body
Yet, I cannot accept his offers
He and I have a broken past
Only God can mend
So I've been fixated on you
The only man I've found worth pursuing
The only person to stimulate me
All of me
I'm not sure that you could love me
Don't think you'd want to try to
Perhaps I only imagined
The electric current flowing through us when our skin touches
I think you're afraid
Scared of what I could become to you
But its not cowardice
It's cautious
Take down your defenses
Let me love you and try your best to reciprocate
You wouldn't regret it
I'd give you everything

I am Better

I am...
A better poet
Though our styles
Are completely different
My talent exceeds yours
A better lover
Because it takes more
Than the physical skills
Of bed-play to make love
A better thinker
Able to consider the possibilities

Evaluate the risks
And make a righteous choice
A better friend
Loyal to my bond
Listening without judgment
Giving comfort and solace
A better person
Able to love unconditionally
Faced with the truth
That love is not reciprocated
And I am too good for you

Preference

Why don't you want me?
I'm beautiful, inside and out
Book smart and street wise
I'm capable of pleasing
Monogamously freaky
But lady-like when it's required
I'm one of the guys
So I could be your best friend
Very talented in more than just the arts
When I love you
When you let me love you
There's nothing that you can't have
If I can give it to you
And loyalty is never a question
I don't believe in loving half way
So you would never be cheated
You should want me!
As a friend, companion
As a lover, a life-mate
But you don't
Not the way that I want you
The question is "why?"
Am I not your preference?

The Enemy in Me

My mind has betrayed me
Folding in on itself
I am no longer in control
Thoughts betray my heart

Deny my intentions
My brain has become the enemy
Striking me with every thought
We are at war
My mind has persuaded my heart
To join the enemy camp
And it is ME against THEM
In the fight to forget him
They have effortlessly gained the upper hand
As I struggle to maintain
Make attempts at common ground
I am losing this fight
But winning small battles
They want to love him
-I already do
And am destroying myself
Trying to forget

Simply, Just, Only Waiting

I am not giving up
Nor have I given in
I have not failed
At least not yet
I am simply waiting...
Living life slow and easy
I am in search of many things
But I'm not looking for love
Not expecting it to find me either
I don't hope anymore
Spent all of my wishes in childhood
I've got my prayers
That's more than enough
Don't believe that love will seek me out
Although I'm not hiding
I am just waiting...
For something more
The type of love that I can feel
The kind that I can see, hear
Touch, taste, breathe, hold tightly
If I had given up
I was not aware
My efforts of adamant pursuit
Halted, frozen at a stare down

Not consistently insisting that he spend time with me
Stopped sending him poetic gifts
I no longer dote on him in plain view
Behave as if unaffected
No, I have not given up...
I am only waiting...
To see if he notices
To see if he recognized the beauty in me
To see if he will realize
The endless possibilities

Process of Creation

Thoughts infinite
Inspiration scarce
In search of something new
Seeking an outlet
Sweet release of creativity
So close to love
Fear would surely be present
Vindicate my mind
Heart is still-framed
A photographic image
Of what it should be
I miss lust
Thought provoking rage
Rough pushing arching
Become alive
Madness consumed
I am the remains
Of two bodies melted
Into liquid lust
Poured into a ceramic mold
Seeking a form of expression
Thus is the process of creating
This poem and this moment

Desired Effect

I am not as good as some claim
I put away my pencil
Tired of writing my wishful lyrics
If I were good
Then why doesn't my poetry soothe him

Why don't my words linger on his mind
And cause his heart to weep with joy
From having been loved
Praised in the form of poetry
Why don't the words cause reciprocation
Provoke hugs and kisses so deep
To cause envy in the angels
Convince him to be in love with me
He reads my words
Remains unaffected
Because I'm not good enough
My poetry isn't good enough
To provoke love
To cause him to desire and reciprocate my affections
I do not want to write
Because my words do not achieve
The desired effect

Private Prayer

Every time I say his name
It is a prayer unto God
I say it aloud
Simply for the sake of hearing it
A sweet song
Sung into my heart
Palms pressed together
I pray
If he's real, let me touch him
Hold him until his hurts
Are no longer in existence
If he's only a glimpse of my dreams
I pray for incessant rest
So that I can be near him
Extended periods of time
I think he might be
What heaven looks and feels like
But if he isn't
I know he must be a close second
And maybe heaven isn't worth being good for after all
Everything about him is poetry
Smooth and delicate
Intimate and intricate
That I could delight in all day

> God, why let me...
> Torture myself?

One-sided: Love

My conviction won't allow me to lie
I've become convinced that I'm insane
Been accused of being in love with you
A man I do not know
But have been intimately connected to
I've felt your pain, shed your tears
Inhaled your intoxicating aroma
Felt when you were near me
Without proof of your presence
Have kissed your mouth
Stood with you in the absence of fear
Made love to you with words
Narrowly etched you into my immortal thoughts
Brushed my lips against your neck
While close in an embrace
You've held me tight to you...
And all for nothing
Just to deny me...
Show me a glimpse of the promise land
Only to prove that it doesn't exist
At least not for me in you
Still, I am unable to lie...
So one day I'll say it aloud
For the sake of my sanity
Putting it on paper does it no justice
To be true to my convictions
Be honest with my heart
I will say it without fear of rejection
In a way that you can comprehend
Gently I will whisper to you
The words kept only in my heart and mind
Softly...
I love you
I love you
I'm in love with you...
God help me I am

Chasing Inspiration

I attempted to catch Inspiration
But he escapes me
At every attempt
To put pencil lead to paper
He dances with the words in my mind
But flees when I make strives to verbalize
His persona
I want to hold Inspiration
Close to me
In the hours when I can't sleep
Comfort my thoughts
Soothe my desires
Cause me to speak
Feel him trace my lips
Provide my words
Deliver me from this cage
Sick with the lackluster
Approach of man's imagination
I need Inspiration to touch me
Guide my hand
Through the process of creation
I need him to make love with me
Out of me
On blank pages

Slight Touch of Insanity

I feel him...
Without having seen him
I feel his presence so strong
That I become physically affected
My body begins to betray me
Stomach turns and knots
Breath becomes shortened
As I attempt to escape
Feeling him coursing through me
Am unable to comprehend
The severity of my condition
I don't understand how I'm able to feel him
How do I know he is near
Without physical evidence?
And the question that is most vexing

May never be answered:
If I can feel him inside of me
Without having seen, smelled, touched, tasted, or heard him...
Can he feel me?
Am I inside of him?
Probably not...
Still, I ponder blindly

Suffer

As soon as I think I'm done
There he is...
The poison slipped into my thoughts
Seeping into me
If I confess the truth
He'll think I'm a fool
If I lie and continue this way
I'm sure I'll go mad
I love him too much to lie
But my pride won't let me be honest
I suffer in private
I want him to want me
Need me, hold me
Soothe me; ease my fears in his eyes...
Love me!
Love me without reason
I would love him until we were no longer
And still more after that
I want to love him
I want to be with him
And I hate that he won't let me
And I hate that he doesn't feel the same
I know better
But I just can't stop wanting him
Even though I want to

Thoughts Gone Wild

A friend of a friend
Of a friend of someone
I know said she saw you...
Riding on the boulevard
Biting you fingernails
For a moment
I wished to be the hangnail
That caused you such distress
To provoke your concern
Enough to draw it into your mouth
Soften the afflicted area
With the careless graze of your tongue
Gently bite, squeeze, and tug
Only to feel the release
Of the agony
Your suffering
Ended in a simple act
As the throbbing eases
Desperately articulating manifestations now!!!
I wish you cared

Writing for Love

I am still trying...
To do the impossible
Carefully craft my words
Into cleverly composed stanzas
Attempt to convey
The depth to which
You have wounded me
Much to no avail
Accepting that my talents
Are mere tools
Proven to be of
Little to moderate use
When it comes to you
Not being provoked
Even to the slightest inclination
Of the possibility
For a desire such as this
I have strived for you

Only to find
Myself struggling
Once more...
Pushing pencil lead to paper
All for the disappointed
Hopes affectionately discarded
Like leaves drifting
Downstream in search of an autumn
That never came
But still I write
In the hopes of a
"One day" and a "maybe"
My words will find your heart
Open and willing
A prayer that I will write love for you
And you will write it back
Feel it back
Give it back
I **WRITE** for **YOU**
Everything else is just an afterthought

Making Words out of Love

I want to make love to you
-With words
Grace your crown with
Soft sounding sighs
Place candy flavored syllables
On your lips
In place of kisses
Whisper the tension out of your shoulders
And caress your neck
With gentle consonants and long vowels
Undress you to the sound
Of a low moan
Long sounding "o"
Tell my secrets to your body
Speak comfort and ease
To your suffering
To your desires
Stroke you with quickening pace
Slowed down only to enunciate
This verbal seduction
As the only way I'm allowed to touch you

I want to touch you
With these tender
Honest, soul bearing words
That you could feel my love
Without me ever having touched you
Close your eyes and
Hear love spoken openly
To the depths that
No touch can reach
The fire that water will not quench
The breath you cannot catch
As easy verbs
Pour down over you
Anticipating the release of your reply
And you say.......?
Well, I'm still waiting-

Parallel

If time could stand still
And every day is just
The replica of the first
Then love would be an imposter
And beauty the imitation of sadness
Life mimics the dream
Time unfreezes
The standards of my obsession
Have yet to be diminished
I, like time, am progressing
But my heart is stunted
Waiting like the pressured coal
Anticipating diamonds
Though I suspect
You may readily give them to another
Some young lover
More appealingly appeasing
Not me
My feelings would be
Neatly put away
With the other hearts you stole
Left to wither into the sour taste
Of love sought after
Still not won
Bitterly loving you all the while

No, my obsession
Has not faded
Rather slightly tainted
From trying to love another
A feeble attempt at replacing you
Though I know there will never be
Another you... for me

The imitation of Love searching for an imitation of Me

Blinded...
When everyone else could see you
The insecure, goofy, imitation
But in my eyes
You were the sugar honey iced tea
To the rest
You weren't even rain water
To a person in the desert
Dying from the lack of H_2O
You meant the world to me
Me and me alone
Only you didn't want me
Although I could love and adore
Comfort and keep
Hold and encase you
Your fragile heart
Creative state-of-mind
I wasn't the one you choose
Not a thing so wrong
That I'd be undesirable
Overlooked and ignored...
Who loves you now?
Loves you better than I could?
I'd like to meet her
If such a woman even exists...
She doesn't
And now I can finally see
You're looking for the imitation of me
(sigh/ chuckle)
GOOD LUCK!
I'm a one-of-a-kind work of art
Anything else is just a fake

One Last Hit

I hear his voice and I am frozen
His image caught in the corner of my eye
Arms pull me in close for an embrace
I am speechless and stunned
Stutter out slow responses to his questions
My mind experiences sensory overload
I long to be free from his gaze
Yet I remain unable to move
Realize that he has stopped my heart
With the complex simplicity of his presence
I can't BREATHE!
Shock my heart out of code blue
It beings to race
Pound against my chest so hard
I hear it in my ears
Am finally able to flee this moment
From the fear of him having heard my speeding heart
Nearly in tears
Struggling to catch my breath
This is not normal!
When he touches me, I'm on fire
I see him and am dazed
Rush home to purge my soul
On my knees in tears
In the dark blue tint of the room
He is my heaven
My mind a personal hell
I pray for deliverance...
I mean nothing to him!
Just a game for his amusement
So why does he mean so much to me?
Why does he cause these sensations in me
And I provoke nothing in him
I do not cause him to feel anything
He does not know me
Doesn't adore me
My name is not his prayer unto God
He does not long for me
Feels no yearning in his heart
So why can't I forget about him?
I fear my sleep for he finds my dreams
And haunts me furthermore

I will not rest my eyes...
I will not be his fool...
At least not after today

Missed His Shout Cue

I was ridiculously hopeless
Holding my heart out
Waiting for him to take it
Wishing he could see me
But his eyes were weak
The days all collided
With my love
His rejection of me
Sweetly dressed in the disguise
Called friendship and respect
His infection spreading
Coursing rapidly through me
The taste of his mouth
Lacking the cure
I was sure would stop the burning
As I flamed without relief
Others knowing
Seeing him as the cheap fix he was
Had no pleasure in him
Saw the guarded
Insecure almost
People pleasing child
I wanted for my own
To love and adore
He lacked for them
The constant appeal
Held for me
They didn't see him
Through my eyes
Couldn't understand my need
The desire
To give him me
This uncommon unshakeable stability
A strong foundation for his home
I could have been
Good for him
Right down to the
Last days of his existence...

He missed the mark
He missed the point of happiness
He let me slip away
Like ice cream
Dripping down the cone
On the 4th of July
And all for what
To live in a world
Where his friends are
Paired off and he leads the life
Solitary and lonely
Rebuking love...
He missed it
I'm already gone

Fool's Gold

He was my addiction
My affliction
My need
I was carelessly seeking
His treasures
Only to find that he
Was nothing more than
Fools gold
He shined like glory
But when tried by fire
He melted away
Into a shallow
Frame of pretence
Not the love that I
Once blindly believed
Him to be
He was a trick
I wanted the illusion
Presented by his words
But he could not deliver

Ended Journey

It hurts...
When the truth is
I shouldn't even be crying
Over him at all
As he was never mine
To begin with
But I wanted him
Love him even
He once said
Something profound to the effect
Silence wasn't
Or wouldn't be
An acceptable solution
Yet he has no words
No response
Conveniently he has
Lost his extensive vocabulary
After reading
Another time about my love...
For him
"I'm in love with you"
Can only be said
In so many languages
So many ways
While I know I shouldn't
That it won't solve anything
Won't make him love me
The tears still scorch my cheeks
And my heart still breaks
Because he still doesn't care
The journey, I fear
Has long been ended

About The Author

Love Her Love Poetry

Dedicated to De'Borah Raquel
By
Michelle Elaine Carter-Wongus
aka Venusdana

I love her poetry like a soothing cry, warm tears filling an ice frozen hollow heart,
Overflowing, overwhelming, overtaking melting the rime from the inside out, bringing back life.
I love her poetry like a battered woman's bitter baggage breaking her back finally tumbling, being trampled beneath her high trodden steps.
Ignoring rational reason, taunting heartache to dive, jump; plunge into love or simply the possibility thereof.
Freedom from the vinegary taste in her mouth, the doubt disabling her throat to swallow love's sweet kiss.
The thought of deception plaguing her mind, placing her on the defensive disappears dissolves into a faint fragrance of hope.
Poetry peaking through the dark clouds, defeating depression, drawing out the truth bringing it into the marvelous light of love that is only found in God and her words.
Where is this stuff that she describes, writes, portrays in her dreams, manifest on paper, and makes the cheating man clean?
Told through an addict's sex laboring out beyond the restrictive womb crushing the most definite boundaries
Her poetry is a high, a struggle to become clean, needing a fix constantly being deterred by the miserable, mundane, monotonous life.
Give me another lyric, another phrase, another word, another poem to read. Never leave me in this world like this, alone without hope of the possibility of love.

www.ingramcontent.com/pod-product-compliance
Lightning Source LLC
LaVergne TN
LVHW051155080426
835508LV00021B/2643